Sol's Daughter

Sol's Daughter

By

Paula Morgan

Publishers • GROSSET & DUNLAP • New York
A FILMWAYS COMPANY

Lyrics on page 77, from the song "It's All Right with Me"
by Cole Porter, from *Can-Can*, copyright © 1953 by Chappell Music.

A letter to a special Daddy
From his daughter
And for all daughters whose fathers have gone

Acknowledgments

A NOTE TO THOSE DEAR
FOR MY DEAR MOTHER WHO MUST STAND SILENTLY
ALONE,
AND MY BROTHER WHO WILL KNOW NOW THE
LONELINESS OF KEEPING HIS OWN COUNSEL,
FOR THE MOST PATIENT HUSBAND TO A WOMAN BORNE,
AND A GEM OF A SON, AND THE DEAREST OF
DAUGHTERS . . . .
TO MY FRIENDS WHO HAVE STAYED THROUGH ALL OF
MY LIFE, AND THOSE LONG STRETCHES OF TIME WHEN
IT SEEMED THAT THE YELLOW BRICK ROAD WAS
LEADING NO WHERE AT ALL, LEAST OF ALL A
RAINBOW. . . .
AND TO STAN REISNER WHO HAD FAITH IN *SOL'S
DAUGHTER* FROM ITS INCEPTION
THE DEAR DAMIOS, WHO SUFFERED THROUGH THE
EARLY LABOR PAINS . . .
TO HAROLD ROTH, AND JACK ARTENSTEIN OF GROSSET
& DUNLAP FOR ALLOWING IT TO HAPPEN,
AND MOST OF ALL TO ROBERT MARKEL . . . WHO WAS
SENT I AM POSITIVE BY MY FATHER TO MAKE SURE
THAT HE WOULD BE IN CHARGE OF ALL OF IT AND
THAT HE ALONE WOULD MAKE IT HAPPEN.

I LOVE YOU ALL . . . . . AND BIG SOL DOES TOO.

Introduction

BIG SOL IS MY FATHER.
HE IS GONE NOW, TO A PLACE I CAN'T SEE, AND TO A
WORLD I KNOW NOTHING ABOUT. WHEN THE ANGEL OF
DEATH TOOK HIM, MY BITTERNESS AND PAIN MADE IT
IMPOSSIBLE FOR ME TO DO ANYTHING BUT WRITE
ABOUT OUR LIFE TOGETHER. IN DOING THIS, MY DAYS
WERE NOT BETTER, ONLY A LITTLE EASIER, BECAUSE I
WAS ABLE TO SUBSTITUTE THE BITTERNESS FOR A
STOREHOUSE OF MAGNIFICENT MEMORIES THAT I
WANTED TO SHARE.

FOR ANYONE WHO HAS BEEN THROUGH THE HELL OF
LOSING, OR FOR THOSE WHO MAY BE SHARPENED BY
THE KNOWLEDGE THAT THIS WILL COME TO ALL OF US,
IN READING SOL'S DAUGHTER, IF FOR A MOMENT THAT
PAIN IS A LITTLE SMOOTHED OVER; THEN INDEED I
HAVE DONE A WONDROUS THING.

I ASKED A HOLY MAN, WHAT COULD I DO TO MAKE MY
FATHER LIVE ON. HE ANSWERED THAT IF I DID GOOD
DEEDS IN HIS NAME THEN HE WOULD LIVE FOREVER.
BIG SOL IS HELPING ME TO DO THAT, AND HOPEFULLY
HELPING YOU.

Paula Morgan

Sol's Daughter

Before

It was a hospital room
An intensive care unit
You lay there
Left arm hooked to a tube nurturing you in some way
Your other hand in mine
A huge hulk of a figure, eyes closed
Your face flushed
Only the strange sounds of monitors could be heard
And my fear!
WE'LL SHOW 'EM, DADDY, WON'T WE?
We always have.
WE'LL CHEAT THE BASTARDS
C'mon, Daddy, I need you.
I need you terribly
FIGHT, DADDY. Fight.
Didn't you always tell me how tough you were?
Fight, Daddy, Please. . . . .
DON'T LET THE LIGHT GO OUT.

I always thought I could maneuver and manipulate
Pull rabbits out of hats.
Even if I didn't know the secrets, or the magic numbers,
I was always the lucky
The one adored,
The one catered to and spoiled and indulged.
I was chosen to have magic in my left pocket . . .
Not anymore, now I am like
So many
A girl without her daddy.
No one to yell at
Or argue with or hang up on
Or even to be giving herring to.

With all of life's gifts before me,
I am now empty. . .
A part of me gone.
Forever gone.
I can't believe forever.
I can't understand that I won't have you anymore.
Why is life so cruel?
Why me
Is it because I have to suffer
Certainly, to know my love.
I cannot bear to plan any tomorrows.
I will never be the same again.
It happens to us all.
But why me?

COULD THE FANTASY BE JUST A LITTLE LONGER?
COULD THE DREAM BE PLAYED ONE MORE TIME!
I do not want comfort,
Only that pain of never forgetting
I am gone, too—
We were the same.
I will live,
But never laugh as I did
Never.
No one will tell me how beautiful I am
In my black velvet.
There are no battles to fight—
But I will live for you, Daddy,
As you would want.
YOU ALWAYS SAID I WAS A SOLDIER.

Death and I have never come to terms.
I understand life.
As I have watched those I love
Leave on the ultimate journey,
For me, they were still here—
Not gone.
Life had a certain foreverness,
An immortality of its own.
I thought as I lived
That nothing ever ended.
It would always stay
But now I know.
I was a child,
A child with fantasies,
Those I loved did go away—
Except in our heads.
I knew then
That I must come to terms with life's devil
And the only way to do it
Was to try to outsmart him;
To live gloriously—
Almost forever
To cheat that bastard who waits with glee—
To take away my fantasy.
No! I will not come to terms with you, Satan!

I WILL BE A CHILD AGAIN,
I LIKE IT BETTER!

None of us is ever prepared for anything, are we!
Are we prepared for birth?
Certainly not our own.
And when the time comes when we give birth,
We take classes and learn about our bodies,
Our pelvises are nature's miracle
And there we are, parents.
No longer children, no . . .
But real parents; images of our own.
The cycle keeps doing its forever number.
We go through all of the madness of parenting,
And then without warning, nature tells us
That our time with what we love is forever gone.

We are not children, really. Not anymore—
We are old and the children are looking to find their nests
Away from us.
As we watch them go, are we prepared for it?
Are we prepared for our own mortality?
We are not!
We prepared for nothing.
We have no philosophy, religion or belief.
We have no heaven.
We have only the hell—
THE HELL OF LOSING what we once thought we had

Forever.
We grasped joy and love for only an instant
And then the angel of death came and took our youth
And our hope.

And so it goes on,
Another day passes,
This one as the last.
Nothing said or done or given,
Though kindly,
Can help.
I am numb.
I feel nothing.
I think empty blue thoughts
And I fear my loneliness.
That voice to tell me stories
Of Europe and the shtetl
The way things were long ago—

It won't matter what I do
Not really.
My big fights are over.
I won all the little battles—
I lost the big one.
Lost him, not to life,
But to a death I knew nothing about.
In a box and in a place unfamiliar to either of us,
He lies there alone, unattended,
Probably cold and as scared as I am,
For the sound of my voice gave him his joy to live.
Our voices will both be silenced,
I AM FORCED TO GROW UP!
No one will call me "baby" anymore—

No one will tell me to call,
No matter what the time . . .
"I worry when I don't hear"
What will I do now?

What advice will I hear from a voice so far away?
Tell me, Daddy.
I AM MORE ALONE THAN YOU
AND SO FRIGHTENED OF THE DARK.

I want sometimes to be where he is—
To get out of my own life
And join him wherever he is.
I HAVE CHILDREN TO RAISE
A LIFE TO LIVE
A MAN TO CARE FOR.
Why does anyone think that anything they can do
Makes it better?
I am angry—
I want to be left alone to share my sorrow with no one—
Not even those who love me most.
They cannot know I have lost my rock.
I feel scared and alone.
The sun will shine tomorrow—
I know that.
My beautiful children will grow
And I will grow old with this man whose life I have chosen
But Daddy, the morning and the night and the days between
Will never ever have that special pulse you gave me!
I will never look for it.
I will never find it because
Only you had it . . .
In the whole world, only you.

I liked the way you looked,
Big and powerful,
With that black, black hair and that chin.
I liked the grand, bigger-than-life personality—
And the way, no matter how much money I needed,

You always sent me an extra twenty-dollar bill
With a clip on the envelope.
Inside the envelope
That said, "In case . . . Daddy"
In print because you couldn't write.
I liked your smile and the way you kept cheating the fates
And holding on, despite all the advice, to that "American
    Dream."

Having a sandwich at three A.M.
Was a banquet with a king.
You knew things
I trusted you and you trusted me—
Absolutely.
TO TRUST COMPLETELY
WHAT A PRIVILEGE.

You made sets in Maine, so I wouldn't ruin my hands—
And carried my picture everywhere so I would be seen.
Your pride in me was known everywhere.
When we went to Europe, no one believed I was your daughter,
Remember?
And where we went and what we shared . . .
We even ate the same way.
Remember?
When I was fifteen, you took me to a diet doctor—
And told him, "I don't ever want her to be fat" . . .
And I never was . . .
You saw to everything—
Your business and your family, your son, Israel and charity.
You always had time for me and the opera
And glamour—
Such strength and power
That is what I will remember and never let fade—
YOU WERE A DREAMER WHO COULD TAKE THAT DREAM
AND WITH YOUR STRENGTH MAKE MIRACLES HAPPEN—
They did.
That's it, Daddy, you were my special miracle.
You still are.

You may be in some alien place, but right now I am smiling.
I am still wearing at this moment
The three-hundred-dollar blue coat
You bought me twenty-five years ago.
"So much money for a coat," Mama said.

I was proud to say "I'm Sol's daughter."
It was a terrific billing . . .
It still is
I AM SOL'S DAUGHTER
Tough and bigger than life.
Aren't I?
Haven't I promised you that a hundred times?
Didn't you always tell me I should have been a boy?
I was an adventurer—
That sometimes you could hardly believe—
That with all the frills and a husband and two children—
I was a girl?
But I am you too
I AM YOUR GIRL

And it is as hard as hell to hear you say in my head

"STOP IT!
I TAUGHT YOU BETTER.
CRYING LIKE THAT.
STOP IT, BABY."

Oh, to hear that again.
Just a minute,
I heard it.

You used to always say
That all you wanted was to keep what you had.
I wanted that more than you
And I would have kept you any way I could
But the mysterious fates were either cruel
Or kind—
I will never know.
Not having you as you were would have been an indignity to you.
I think you knew better than any of us
That your time was up.
You were trying to prepare me
I knew that.

And yet, I liked reporting to you—
As if I were only the corporal
And I knew that you were the captain.
I am only carrying out those jobs
You taught me well to do.
But what you forgot to teach me
Was not having your big hand in mine.
You didn't tell me about that.

How my heart would jump when I saw you waiting
At an airport or in your big chair for me.
Or waiting at those incredible train stations
Any hour, any city, when I was touring.
You would be there to feed me more than I needed,
Find me a big bath, brush me off
And start me again.

Nothing was too big for you.
That was your job, captain.
EVERYTHING SEEMS TOO BIG FOR ME NOW—
I AM STILL ONLY A CORPORAL.
I needed you to graduate me—
I needed your special diploma to make it seem
As if in some way I could take your place.
I can't.
I can still only carry out orders
And hope that I can remember everything you taught me to do.
You taught me so much, but not how to cheat the inevitable.
You taught me how to get whatever I wanted.
You had such style.
But, me . . .
I am without a captain—
With only those orders left in my head—

The day you were put to rest I looked at Mama
So small,
Unable to understand what she was losing,
Her past,
Her present, her future.
You were not a husband or a father or a man with magic—
You were a life.
The day the fates took you, she said
"THE CURTAIN IS DOWN"
"THE EPIC IS OVER"
My God!
You had been together over half a lifetime—
She is tragic;
She wanted you back any way
She cannot find a chair to sit on or a bed to lie in.

You and she, a story.
Two people from the bottom of Europe's ghettos
Coming together, and making life work.
You loved her so.
And, though she found it hard to show
She respected what you were
Such beautiful people—
I always thought you were both exactly the way it was supposed
    to be.
She forever learning, and you, building and building.
I never saw you two in the poses children see parents in—
I saw you as

Two sculptured pieces
Mama like a black onyx cameo and you a hero—
All shiny and full of dreams
"America, America"
THE HOLOCAUST KILLED YOUR SHINE.
I DON'T REMEMBER WHEN I FIRST NOTICED,
THERE WASN'T THE KIND OF LAUGHTER THAT THERE USED
    TO BE.

I loved you both so—Mama letting me think
I was first. I was not—you had room enough for all of us.
But I have come to believe the real truth
She was first; she was your lady best.
I had a special place, but it wasn't hers.
Hers was that of a friend, wife, lover and partner.
I remember when you bought her that beautiful black coat
And hung it on the door when she was still in the hospital.
I remember those romantic things you did—
Things we didn't speak about,
You are what I think it is
I have never seen it ever
That kind of devotion.
It didn't show to the world
But I knew it because I looked.
You were different, brought together by a great tragedy.

When I was very little you took me to a big photographer
On Wilshire with my brown braids and had me photographed—
Dressed from Bullock's Wilshire
As if I were a princess
I BELIEVED THAT I WAS—
YOU TOLD ME SO MANY TIMES.
And the first words to a stranger were always,
"See, doesn't the baby look good."
In that accented voice.
I BELIEVED IT A LOT—
BELIEVED IT WHEN A CRUEL WORLD SAID NO A MILLION
    TIMES—
I was your princess—
And you would say—
    "YOU GOT A CONTRACT WITH ME FOR LIFE."

Whose life, Daddy, yours or mine?
I went to some sort of service where Biblical things were said
I saw it and I heard it
But I don't for one minute believe it
How could that be
That you would leave me alone.
And yet, I know
I will remember and smile and laugh and tell stories about you
All my life.
NO ONE WILL EVEN THINK I AM ANNA KARENINA . . .
I am just one more person,
But that was your secret.
YOU MADE ME ALWAYS FEEL SO SPECIAL.

It's harder now because I am cold
And this is a hard adventure.
I used to watch fascinated starting at eight; in your office
The battles you won to save your precious business
I thought you were the greatest entertainer, and
I learned very early how to handle those gangsters
That would take away what you worked for.
I learned, yet I didn't even know what I was watching, until
     now.

Just yesterday a card came with your name on it;
Some sort of credit card.
Even in death you are still trying to protect me.
I won't believe it and maybe it will go away
Like the bad dreams I used to have as a child.
I used to jump between you and Mama in that big bed
And I would find my rest.
Now the bad dream won't go away
I try hard, but I can't get out of the house
I don't want to
It's a kind of Shiva I'm sitting
Just my own.
YOU USED TO SAY THAT GOD SMILED AT ME ANYWHERE
HE CERTAINLY ISN'T SMILING AT ME NOW
Maybe I am being punished
I don't know anything.
I thought as long as I had you around I could beat everything
I am not so knowing

There's not a minute of smart inside of me
For the first time, I am frail
I want to hide
But that's not your daughter, is it, Daddy?
That is someone else
So frailness has to be kicked out
No more tears today
BUT THERE ISN'T ANYONE TO GIVE
MY TERRIBLE FOOD TO.

A man has a special love for a son.
A son is his immortality.
Whether the son is like him or not, he adores him.
He was favored too, wasn't he, Daddy?
A frail child who coughed and played the violin
Recited and had those curls!
He was your favorite for a long time.
And near the end I think you enjoyed each other a lot.
You both talked politics and about Europe and man things.
He drove you, and tended, I know you thought him kind,
Intelligent—but I WAS THE SOLDIER.

His brain was for bigger pursuits
He a philosopher, not a materialist.
I think in your heart you liked that.
He was an idealist; that was hard for you to swallow,
But you did, and accepted him as he was.
You loved him in a special way
I never really understood.
Now I do, I think.
"OUT OF EGGS COME DIFFERENT CHICKENS" Bubbe would
    say . . .
But we both came from both of you, so there must be something
We share.
We'll find it, Daddy.
Losing you has made us closer
You wanted us to be friends and I promised you.
I'll keep my promise.

When I was a girl in New York, you came to see me, your student,
How everyone waited to be asked to lunch or dinner
How proud I was to have a father that looked like you . . .
Who had an extra buck and didn't care who he spent it on.
That was best.
"Girls, this is my father"—I would say it extra loud,
You went down the street saying,
"I'm Paula's father, she must owe you money" . . .
And I did.
The cleaner and the tailor and the baker . . .
You used to go into every store near the Barbizon
Just knowing I owed money
It was charming,
You were fun.

In these later years, you would tell me, "Baby, I'm not forty
Anymore," and I would not listen.
To me you were always the same until yesterday.
And then
Yesterday my heart stopped
I was slowed
My step weakened
My childhood over
My little girl will only remember a memory
And my son a scream in terror,
After all, you raised him most of all.
You had such plans
He will carry them out, but poor thing, he is so confused

So battered, so unable to focus.
You were his rock
But he now has his own father to get those special nutrients from
They will be good.
What you would have been able to give was a world long gone.

It's hard for him,
He thought you were immortal
I cannot fathom the thoughts of a husband
Who has shared his wife with another man
Even though the man is her father
His pain is obvious
And how does he handle those things that were so much a part
    of her
Where does he go now?
To whom does he turn
His is the ultimate responsibility
He must be everything
The family will look to him to provide with love, and stories
That special care.

Remember Husband, how our son wouldn't eat for us
And we sat outside our house waiting until Grandpa soothed
And burped him . . . weren't those days wonderful?
In that ghastly tone, the special sound that loving fathers sing
And to burping boys—"Over the Rainbow"—I hear that in my
    ears
REMEMBER, GRANDPA would go home wet
With baby smells and sweat, only to come again the next day

All over again.
Remember, Husband?

HOW QUICKLY YOU became a grandfather
When yesterday, you were an immigrant with a dream.
And how Grandma took our son to the park to run and play
Only to return him to YOU DADDY, for the forever feedings.

It was a lovely play,
I think we went to Disneyland everytime we could
Our days were endless Disneyland, weren't they?
DID YOU WANT ME, HUSBAND, TO BELIEVE THAT LIFE WAS
    DISNEYLAND?
DID YOU WANT TO KEEP REALITY AWAY TOO?
IS THAT WHY YOU WERE CHOSEN TO TAKE CARE OF THIS
    PARTICULAR FLOCK?

The nurse who was in charge of tiny Lisa Beth was enormous.
Her voice booming,
She would only hand the tiny baby to you,
Your hands like hams and she knew that,
And in an instant you were at your post feeding and changing
Daring to let the nurse bathe this special baby,
Your first and only granddaughter.
You and the nurse fought
And then we let her go because you were the best nurse
You were the best everything, weren't you?
You could handle a baby, and a spoiled girl, a smart wife
A dreamlike grandson with burps and fears of the dark—
And banks and businesses and loan sharks.
You were just able—
A GIANT.
Everyone thought you were
That is why our shock is so great
We believed, like Moses, you would not disappear from us
Until we were ready.

Everyone had their own special romance with you
But none like mine.
I won't let anyone have that but me.
Except Mama. I will allow that.
REMEMBER I AM SELFISH LIKE YOU
I WANT THE WHOLE COOKIE.

Why can't I have it the way it was?
Will life ever let me forget what a lonely girl I really am?

That no one, no matter how much he knows,
WILL KNOW PERETZ OR BIALIK.
OR *DAS KAPITAL* OR SMOKE A CIGAR LIKE YOU OR WEAR A
    RED SHIRT.
DADDY, TALK TO ME, PLEASE.
I'M WAITING.

My first memory of you, I think, is sitting in your big bed
Sundays and having you read the funnies to me.
I must have been very little because my pajamas had a drop seat
And feet connected to them.
I wonder if daddies read funnies anymore.
In my house there isn't any real Sunday
Sunday school starts so early,
We went to Orthodox Saturday school
And Sunday mornings were lazy.
You used to read me the Katzenjammer Kids and Popeye
Weren't those the days of innocence?
Another world
It is strange that we all know that we grow old
But we rather don't notice it . . .
Maybe it's because we don't want to
BUT I KNOW I DON'T WEAR DR. DENTON'S ANYMORE
AND I CAN'T REMEMBER IF PAPERS EVEN HAVE THE
     FUNNIES.

We had such a colorful house,
Because everyone lived so interrelated.
Remember when I used to go to cotillions and the whole street
Used to come and look at me in my formals.
No one went from our neighborhood, only me—
I was a little embarrassed about it.
You used to say "what difference the neighborhood?
We'll move when your mother will let us
YOU'RE GOOD ENOUGH FOR ANYONE."
That was put in early.
That I was good enough for anyone.
That is what I should thank you for most.
Giving me so much self-worth, that even if I wasn't,
It wouldn't have mattered because you made me believe—
NOT TO BE AFRAID EVER OF ANYONE LOFTIER OR SMARTER
    OR RICHER THAN I
Only be afraid of those dangers that pretty girls fall prey to
You talked to me a lot about that.

We were a real family
We fought a lot and we were growing like people
So many different kinds of people
Like neighborhoods all over America
Our house had an air.

When I was little everyone in our neighborhood
Looked like working people except YOU.
YOU looked like a Russian hussar and our house,

We had everything we were supposed to have—
Bunk beds and a door from your and mother's room
That went out to a garden—
We weren't rich, but we had a lot.
And the lovely old lady who took care of me
I think she was a hundred when she came
And two hundred when she left us.
Her name was Mrs. Dolly, and you took her to her Catholic
    services
Every Friday, didn't you,
There were Erlene and Domingo who worked in the store
And drove us and Jesús, and Sarah who ironed
And we had lessons
Didn't we.
I hated Hebrew, but I went, 'til you told me I didn't have to.
And Mr. Perlmutter taught us Hebraic philosophy
And it was like that in houses everywhere, in our special
    space.

Mama made sure we had culture
You provided, whatever men are supposed to
I never missed anything, did I.
The best of everything! I learned room service early
Peach ice cream in the vestibule on the Santa Fe Super Chief.
Going to New York.
Everything was always Super Chief, wasn't it.
You jumped on Ambassador flights to New York as easily as
    some
People go to the corner

Always more for me, coats, dresses and love
Elegant people who played music and read poetry and spoke lan-
    guages
Political things and a house of pride.
THAT'S THE LEGACY, DADDY
I COME FROM A HOUSE OF PRIDE.

You always told me how handsome you were as a youth in
    Poland
That you were Valentino
I thought you were John Garfield
Women adored you; but, you were not the gallant Don Juan—
You were always putting me in front of you when the ladies
    pursued—
How funny.

So many family responsibilities
Sisters who didn't marry
And brothers who couldn't work
And Jews. All the Chasids in the world were in our store!
Never saw so many Rabbis
A SON WHO WAS ALWAYS GOING TO SCHOOL
A WIFE WHO WAS SAVING THE WORLD FOR DEMOCRACY
A DAUGHTER WHO THREW MONEY AROUND
As if it were not currency but a toy
No, a Don Juan you never were,
You took me everywhere with you

And told me stories of your youth
And the early anti-Semitism in Poland and how you knew
To get out
And that lesson was:
"BABY, ALWAYS KNOW WHEN IT IS NOT A SAFE PLACE FOR
    YOU"
"TRUST YOURSELF"

"LEARN TO SMELL IT"
"LEARN TO KNOW WHERE YOU BELONG"
"IF YOU DON'T LIKE IT, GET OUT"
"IF THEY ARE GIVING IT AWAY AND IT'S NOT FOR YOU,
    THEN DON'T TAKE IT"
"NO ONE DOES A FAVOR WITHOUT SOMETHING BACK"
"ALWAYS HAVE AN EXTRA BUCK . . . YOU'LL NEED IT"
"BE STREET SMART, BUT NOT OF THE STREET"
"NOTHING CAN BUY YOU NOTHING"

I went to New York and
I walked all alone
Trying to walk New York in your steps
What was once Ellis Island and Brooklyn and Coney Island,
I took some strange subway to Queens.
I didn't know where I was . . . I just wanted to walk there
Where you had when you first came,
I found myself on a Staten Island ferry
It was cold and raining . . . it didn't matter
I wanted to try to feel what you could have felt.
It was dramatic, but I couldn't possibly know what
Ignorance and poverty felt like.

I then went to the Barbizon and down Third Avenue and up
    Lexington
I had been in New York a hundred times, but Daddy was always
At the other end of the phone waiting to talk to me
Not this time!
I would not call from the pay phone outside saying
"Daddy, I'm safe"
I could call Mama and my family, but the catch in that voice
Would be gone.

So I walked into our places, not yours and Mama's
Because the Yiddish theatre was gone
And Moscowitz and Lupowitz was no longer
Canal Street wasn't the same
But I was warm in a big mink coat, that you gave me—not as
    young
And in remembrance I could feel the tears on my cheeks,
You and Mama had to have such love to come so far and to New
    York
And then even further to San Francisco
Then because my brother coughed, you came to hot Los Angeles
It was good for coughing only children
Oh, Daddy
What an adventure
And the tiny lady beside you
You talk of my courage,
I have none
Not really
I am only a small vessel of what you both were together
Your story so romantic
To start from the very bottom
Built for us a castle.

My children will know the stories but they won't hear all
Those sounds of languages being spoken
They won't see a *Forvetz* or a *Tag*
They will know through their own eyes what they come from
But the color that I had, never . . .
Poor children
Deprived of that legacy
Bible wisdom and of anecdotes . . .

You were never a nothing, Daddy
You didn't have a lot when you came,
You used to tell me that you bought second-hand suits
But the best, "BETTER AN OLD GOOD ONE, THAN A NEW
    CHEAP ONE"
You used to say
And I swallowed everything you said and believed you
Would talk to me forever. Won't you, Daddy?
I think you did promise that to me
No, I know you did.
Talk to me.

I never tired of hearing about Danzig and Europe before
Hitler took it and Russia cut it up.
Tell me stories about when the czar traveled, Daddy
Tell me that guards were standing at each railing not like
In America where Presidents go without bubble tops
Tell me that Daddy
And about Mother's troika and the Polish winters
And your grandfather who had a farm and your mother who
    came
From a good family . . . tell me, I want to hear it again.
Tell me about your youngest sister who had eyes like mine
That haunted you until your last day, tell me, Daddy
I have no one to wake up and tell me those marvels
No one knows that, Daddy
Only you
AND NOW I CAN'T HEAR YOU.
MAYBE WE HAVE A BAD CONNECTION, DADDY
I'M WAITING, DADDY
I'M WAITING.

Maybe my loss is so hard because it is so much
A father can be nice and good and a father
But a grandiose gentleman is something else.
I remember living at the St. Regis in New York for a month once
And you telling the room service people not to forget to put
A yellow rose on the tray if and when I ordered

And all the times you said
"GIVE HER WHAT SHE WANTS, I'LL TAKE CARE OF IT"
ALL OF THAT INDULGENCE GONE
ALL OF THE STORIES, EXCEPT IN MY HEAD
MY INSOMNIA WAS REALLY THERE SO THAT I COULD HEAR
    YOU IN THE NIGHT
AND NOW I WAKE BUT I DON'T HEAR
HOW DO I HANDLE THAT
DADDY, TELL ME A STORY.

Today is the kind of day you liked
Misty, foggy and cool
You just didn't like the sun—you said it made your face hurt
But how many times did you put me in the sun
To cure my not getting a part or a broken heart!
Didn't Mother always say that you were ruining me
That there wouldn't be a man that could ever take your place!
How right . . . ruin, I don't know—
Take your place
Never
Gruff, but dear
Holler, but wonderful!

We loved the Clift Hotel in San Francisco
And how the wind battered our faces
We loved Israel too
The outside tea drinking places where we could watch people
And delicatessens
Lox and cream cheese on a bagel:
It was your signature.

I just realized that you bought me my first pack of cigarettes
Although you hated it

"Parliaments"
I'm not much of a smoker, but I smoke nothing else
I remember, too, that you weren't afraid of taking me into bars
And teaching me about liquor and Las Vegas
And the perils of gambling
I don't know if it was a lesson
I just know that I don't like liquor and gambling
Is for suckers
A lot of lessons you were teaching to a girl
Before it was considered OK

You used to always say
"DO WHAT YOU WANT . . . MAKE YOUR OWN CHOICES"
"YOU BE IN CHARGE"
Telling a girl all that so early
No wonder that I couldn't find a place for myself for so very long
I thought the whole world was like you
I really did!
You were what I thought men were; that I would be always
Treated as you had . . .
You know that was wrong, Daddy, terribly wrong!
The world was not you, not at all
I found a few people
But not with your grace

I tried hard but I just couldn't find it
That only exists in a European boy glad to be alive in
America and wanting very very hard to succeed.
Americans don't have that—it is not in their nature
Food and life here are too easy
You never spanked me or hit me.
But you didn't like eye shadow or the way I began to look
If I were out too late or I smoked with the wrong people.
You trusted me, but not the world.
You loved and hated the thought that men would look at me
And approve or disapprove of me when I started to want to be
An actress
You wanted me famous, but innocent
You wanted me stared at but not desired
You were as silly as I was
We were in a world we had mixed feelings
About, a world where sex and men were the commodities
And you wanted me to have all of that without the other part
How naive we were, weren't we?
You had that too
Naiveté.

I used to wonder how you
Lived through so much

Will there ever be anything like you again
I doubt it
The new men are not like you
I think your generation had that
Only some throwback maybe will be in love with
Jewish music as you were and ritual though you didn't believe it
And food
How you loved food and the sounds of a Cantor
REMEMBER "VANDER YICH ALEIN"

Do you know if I clocked the hours we talked on the phone
The clocks would have to start a whole new way of timing them-
    selves
I think that is my greatest sorrow
Not to have taped all of that
To keep
THE WAY YOU TOLD ME HOW YOUR FATHER, RELIGIOUS AS
    HE WAS,
KEPT HAVING CHILDREN, HUNGRY CHILDREN, AND YOU
    HAD TO SUPPORT
THEM AT THE AGE OF TEN. YOU knew how to make a living
    always
Tell me, could my kids do that?
No.
It's all too easy for them
All taken care of
Maybe they won't have to
But I never ever met men who had it all easy who really were
Anything—never ever
I think I found that out from you
And the way you treated your mother.
At eighty, or whatever, you wanted her to look beautiful
And when we had a little money, she always had black patent
    leather
Shoes and looked like a queen
You wanted us to be people out of pages
Not real people
I think that was your fantasy

And with that truth gone
Now we are only people
PEOPLE ALONE WITHOUT THAT SPECIAL SHINE THAT YOUR
    GLOW THREW TO US
That line . . .
"BABY, DON'T WORRY, IT WILL BE OK"
"I'M HERE, I'LL TAKE CARE OF IT"
But you are not here, Daddy, and I have to take care of it
I have help, sure, but it isn't you.
In their way everyone tries . . . I know that
But, today I started making a roast
You know how I loved to cook my lousy way for you
But it won't be what it would if you were eating it!

MY HAND WAS IN YOURS WHEN THAT DAMNED FATE TOOK
    YOU FROM ME
I STILL FEEL IT
A HAND THAT COULD KNOCK YOU ACROSS A ROOM WITH
    SUCH A HELLO
And so many little things . . .
Like a watch in a candy box on Valentine's Day with chocolate
Covered cherries in the box
And, though you hated Christmas because I loved it, there was
Chanukah gelt in the stocking
You let me have dogs too
Animals that cost time and money and pain and I remember
    when
Our cocker Cleo bit a postman and you hid him in your big store
So that they wouldn't take her away
That too you let me have
I remember when I took the kids one summer to Idyllwild and
You sent us so much meat that those racoons invaded us . . .
"SO I SHOULD HAVE ENOUGH"
"SO I SHOULDN'T BE HUNGRY"
"SO IT WOULD BE OK"
Will it ever be OK again?
Will it ever smile the way you did on all of us?
Will we know real joy?
We're going to try like hell!
And we'll go through the motions
Maybe I'll wake up and it will all be a bad, bad dream
But that is silly
It has happened
And I sit here trying to put it all down so that my

Children who will grow to remember you at times will have it
Strongly in their hands
THAT HE WAS NOT A GRANDFATHER OR A FATHER OR A
  HUSBAND
BUT A MAN THE WAY MEN ARE SUPPOSED TO BE
AND MY KIDS COME FROM THAT STRENGTH AND THAT
  FIGHT AND THAT ABILITY
It is the only way I know to give myself some feeling of comfort.

When banks changed to computers, you said, "WHY IS A MAN'S
    HANDSHAKE NOT ENOUGH?"
For you it always was.
You took everything at its word!
Even when I had to lie and you knew it you made me think I was
Telling the truth
You thought you could buy a lot of freedom and you did
How do I tell that to my kids?
You always said "GIVE A GUY SOME DOUGH AND YOU'LL
    ALWAYS GET
A ROOM AND A TICKET . . . DOUGH IS THE CHEAPEST THING
    THAT YOU HAVE TO GIVE."
"IT MEANS NOTHING BECAUSE IT ISN'T HUMAN."
I never will forget that.
You went through so many crises with money and yet
You never ever let me think I was poor
I always thought I was the richest girl I ever knew
I wanted to be Rockefeller's daughter in my fantasy
I imagined that I was
But when I thought about it I
Wanted only to be YOUR daughter and that is still the best
I sit here smiling and weeping and thinking
Your mortality is me and your son and our kids
And that part of you that we shove into them
But I think I am your biggest part
It will give me sanity
And a way to fight this horrible depression that comes in
Waves like a permanent nausea.

"YOU ARE MY BEST PIECE," you would say to me
THAT'S APPROVAL
THAT'S WHY I CAN BE KNOCKED ON MY ASS AND GET UP
    AND WALK
BECAUSE IT COMES TO ME
"WHO'S KNOCKING?"
"AND WHO ARE THEY?"
AND YOU USED TO SAY TO ME
"WHY, BABY, YOU THREW MORE MONEY AWAY LAST YEAR
    THAN THAT GUY
WILL EVER MAKE . . . YOU ARE CRYING BECAUSE HE SAID
    NO."
"GOOSE THAT YOU ARE
YOU'RE SOL'S DAUGHTER"
AND I AM!

I guess there are daughters that hate their fathers
I assume looking at the statistics that men leave their daughters
To fend for themselves.
To work life the best they can
And when death comes to those fathers maybe the tears are shed
For other reasons but a lot of ladies I know are exactly like us
They didn't have Sol. Maybe
But they had something like it and it's terrible
But to remember is wonderful.

I don't know how you had the time to see me every play I was
Ever in and make a living.
You were always the only father in the auditorium; sitting on a
Hard hot seat in the middle of the day
Waiting for his third grade star to make her entrance
And all the things my children were in, at those tiny school
Auditoriums, you were there
If we had a line or a song or a story
Whatever
You were always there as if it were a premier
The other day a friend told me that you once left a big meeting
To pick me up from a beauty shop
I asked the person who told me and he said that
You seemed to enjoy doing the big little something to make
A daughter's heart bounce and want it forever.
We daughters want it from our husbands.

HUSBANDS AREN'T FATHERS
THEY HAVE A DIFFERENT POSITION
THEY ARE SUPPOSED TO BE EXTENSIONS
IT MUST BE IMPOSSIBLE
IT IS.

Your temper was not terrific; it was a fault
But such a softie after the big grumble
That is what you gave everyone
A special kind of comfort
Freud says we're supposed to grow out of father love at about
Twelve
Bullshit
You can't grow out of love at any age because you're supposed to.

You taught me
I know things
You even took me to a burlesque show once so I would hate it
I did
And the theatre
The plays you let me see when I wasn't supposed to!
I saw *Rain* when I was ten!
And the disdain you taught me about hating other religions
You used to say
"They all got something
All of 'em"
They are all good teachers
"It wouldn't hurt you to know about a lot of things"
You weren't too happy about the churches I made you walk
    through
In England
You thought they ought to have some heat!
IF SHELLEY WERE SO GREAT, YOU SAID, WHY WAS THE
    PLACE SO COLD . . .

YOU HATED WHAT THE WAR HAD DONE TO YOUR JEWS
YOU THOUGHT YOU WERE RELATED TO ALL OF THEM
AND IN THE LATER YEARS WHEN THE ASSASSINATIONS
 CAME
YOU KEPT SAYING:
"THEY AREN'T WATCHING"
"PEOPLE DON'T CARE"
"WHAT'S WRONG WITH A GOVERNMENT THAT ALLOWS
 SUCH LIBERTIES" . . .
You loved America
She was your mistress
You loved what she gave you
You always worked for yourself
Being your own boss in your own business
Even tiny, it was yours!
Your own boss making your own decisions
I remember the money drawer
It was a drawer in your desk
And I would take it, or whoever needed it, and even when the
 store
Had hard times, we always knew you could get us out of any-
 thing.

 I THOUGHT YOU WOULD BEAT THE RAP
 I THOUGHT YOU WOULD BE OK
 I DID NOT FORESEE DEATH
 I WAS SURE THAT WHEN THE EVENTUAL DAY CAME, I
 WOULD KNOW IT FIRST
 WHAT A COLOSSAL EGO YOU GAVE ME

THAT I COULD THINK I WOULD KNOW
BUT YOU DID IT, DADDY.

I don't know what I believe
I think I am just like everyone else but I had a better time for
Longer, didn't I?
You could turn a plain Tuesday into New Year's Eve
And you did
I loved going to Hollywood with you,
And the funny counter at Musso Franks where we met all
The important Hollywood writers and we talked to them
And I loved your languages
You could speak everything, but your English had a
Special careful sound of someone who learned it late.
I loved that.
And your signature on a check that never bounced.
I can remember going on rides with you in
The nights when sleep would not come
The energy, the veal cutlets with egg on top
And I think the conversation
Was the best
Talking and listening to big men raising money for Israel
When Israel was
Declared a state and I got into Madison Square Garden
On the stage singing the national anthem
On the Movietone news, I knew you and Mama would be proud.

YOU TAUGHT ME TO LIE WHEN I HAD TO
TO KNOW WHAT TRUTHS WERE IMPORTANT AND WHAT I
    COULD GLOSS OVER
TO YOU THERE WAS NO TRADITION
THERE WERE RULES . . . JUST DECENCY AND HONOR
AND ONE'S OWN WORD
YOU USED TO SAY IF YOU GIVE YOUR WORD, THAT'S ENOUGH

How the theatre attracted you.
You wanted it for yourself but there wasn't any money in it
And it wasn't nice for a boy from Chasids to be an actor
You loved it
I think that's why it happened for me
You did it through me
And I did it first for you and then somehow we had a bond
The interminable waits that you had with me outside theatres!
You would say to me "TELL THOSE FOOLS YOUR FATHER IS
    TAKING YOU HOME.
YOU DON'T NEED A RIDE, NOT FROM ANYONE, OR A DINNER
YOU CAN BUY YOUR OWN."
How independent you tried to make me
And, Daddy, this was before any women's movement
You didn't want me to be used as women had been in the theatre
The thought of it would have killed you
And I knew and walked fast and far away from temptation.
You used to tell me it would show on my face
And maybe you were right.
Here I am a grown woman with children of my own and life

Shows on my face but not the life that you would not have
   wanted
For me
Nothing cheap
"YOU'RE NOT FOR SALE, DO YOU HEAR ME, BABY
THE OTHERS MAY BE, BUT NOT YOU"

I am lonely
I will be all of my life, won't I
Every day there will be less pain, the experts say
Will there?
And Mama, I am so afraid for her!
And your son
My Brother
"YOU CAN BE ANYTHING YOU WANT" you would say to me
"ANYTHING"
The BIGGEST SEATS
The MOST CANDY
The RIDE ON THE ELEPHANT . . . what other kid did I know
Whose daddy bribed the man to let her ride the elephant.

MOVIES WERE FOR TRAMPS.

BUT THE THEATRE . . . you wanted me to be something
wonderful

DO *MEDEA*

REMEMBER IN GREECE WHEN WE SAW *MEDEA* AND YOU
TOOK ME TO THE

ACROPOLIS AND TOLD ME ABOUT DEMOCRACY AND
SOPHOCLES AND ARISTOTLE

HOW DID YOU KNOW ALL THAT WHEN YOU NEVER WENT
TO A SCHOOL?

HOW DID YOU KNOW TO TELL ME ALL THOSE THINGS

You knew something about every city we were in.

You even took me to Parliament

And the Knesset

The applause when you walked in

When I saw your name in the Herzl Museum I almost fainted

My father

A colossal showman

Wherever we went

You knew people and they knew you

Rabbis, doctors, politicians and businessmen

Everyone knew you and loved you and I was always so damn
happy

To walk just next to you.

You worried about my chicken pox and your son's broken leg
and

The SLAUGHTER OF THE INNOCENT.

Now who can tell me anything except what I remember in my
head?

YOU KNEW BLACK PERFORMERS
TOOK ME AT THIRTEEN TO HEAR THEM
AND YOU NEVER LET ME DISCUSS COLOR . . . EVER
BECAUSE YOU WERE A HUMANITARIAN
Mother coming from such refinement
She had tutors and culture and her father wore a silk hat
And went to the opera and her family was rich!
And you vowed to make us the way Mama's people were before
    they
Took poison so Hitler wouldn't rape their bodies and burn their
Houses! WHEN WARSAW FELL TO THE GERMANS, YOU DIED
    THOSE DEATHS
SO MANY TIMES. I REMEMBER MAMA'S TEARS THROUGH THE
    WALLPAPER
I was tiny
I didn't ever understand any of that until I grew up and then
I never trusted God anymore . . I told you that I never trusted
Religion, only money and power
I was never afraid as long as you were there.
I didn't have any respect for money, but I knew it could buy
One's way out of a ghetto or into a heaven

Your time had very quickly come.
Too quickly for us to know what it has done to us.
Your life had such suffering because you pulled out every stop
And you couldn't save enough Jews, you always said
You couldn't and how hard you tried.
Nothing after was ever really important
You weren't like the usual men who had hobbies or women or
    played

Cards. You were dedicated to us and to a humanity that you hoped
  To help in some way. That was all.
And you did the job the very best.
THERE ARE FATHERS AND THERE ARE FATHERS
I still remember
How you had to beg the algebra teacher to pass me so I
Could get into college

And the visas you could get. To come to America,
Because you learned how to find the people who could forge
The right papers and get out of Germany.
That was your talent—to find anything.
The trip was awful
Thirty-one days on the boat but you knew that Mother loved her
Hair and, at Ellis Island, you saw to it she wasn't
Embarrassed like the other women. She would keep her hair
And her dignity.
That's what you gave us . . dignity
You must have been born with that.
She always said that Daddy has a way with life.
He'll fix it . . . and you did!
You got a job right away in New York for a lot of money and
Sent money home to your mother . . after a few weeks you
Saved enough to get on a train to San Francisco
You didn't like the poverty in the streets of New York and
In California there was gold in the streets. Yes, Daddy, there was
And you found it.
I never really remember not having . . .
Only having

I remember Mama wouldn't live in Beverly Hills because
It wasn't near a Kosher butcher . . I remember all of that.
And the way you strutted when you finally bought that big
    building

The building is here, Daddy,
And you would be happy to see it.
Clean painted, and occupied.
That is what you wanted to leave us with—your precious
    building
To me it was only a huge headache of cement but to you it was
"AMERICA, AMERICA" and who could quarrel with that.

As I look outside my window, the day ending
Tomorrow seems a long way away even though today is almost
    at end
Will I miss you less tomorrow, Daddy?
Will I forget anything!
You know that passage . . "IF I FORGET THEE O JERUSALEM . .
MY RIGHT ARM SHOULD LOSE ITS CUNNING."
I have no cunning in me anymore
I am still in need and though I sound smart, I'm not
I have lost my best friend.
I have lost my heart.
And I stay cold
I turned on the roast and cleaned the kitchen and I sip very hot
    tea
And my children will soon be home. Their young smiles bright.
And the night will come
My husband will give me his heart as best he can
But my aloneness will follow me into the night.

Good friends will keep calling and coming.
New people will come into my days.
But they will never know that my need for you hasn't changed
Since the first time you turned on the light and told me I didn't
Have to sleep in the dark. Not ever.

It isn't just love that I have known
Or passion. But it is unselfish love, the kind that great people
Write about.
What people were there then? . . Only you two
There aren't love stories like that anymore except in books
Special books written long ago when men and women were
    heroic.
That's what you both were . . heroic.

You never sold in a store, not even your own, it wasn't your way.
You had a special arrogance that you gave to me
Particularly to me
And what trouble that has caused me.
You never used your power, though you knew how.
You never lived from anything but your own head and hands
And people worked for you forever.
It was like that.
Even now.
In these empty lonely days.

It is impossible to tell you how many people call and write to me.
It's as if you were a President or something.
You were my president.

You gave me special powers.
I am afraid I won't have that quite anymore.
Not that way.
When Ben Gurion died I remember that you said Israel will
Be different because he was old and tired but he set the right
Path.
That's what you did, Daddy, you set the right path.
And you were always yourself.
Wherever you were was big and bright and magnanimous.

In my mind's eye right now I see you in a black tuxedo
So young and handsome and Mama in red chiffon
And I see the pose forever in my head,
A woodcut in my brain.
I never really saw you old.
Sometimes it would bother me how your step faltered.
But—I would push it away as if it weren't there
It was my talent, to push it away.
You didn't teach me that
I just found it
It made getting older easier for both of us.
And how you kissed my hand only a week ago.
Will I not feel that again?
Will I not know that soft mouth on my freckled hand?
Gallant, that was it,
I never saw such charm. YOU USED TO SAY THAT CHARM WAS
     A VERY
NECESSARY INGREDIENT FOR LADIES. But for me.
In my own life
YOU GAVE ME AMMUNITION.
It is almost as if I were going to run General Motors.
Did I need all of that? Did I,
Didn't you ever tire of Me?
I bet you did.
I bet I exhausted you with my myriad of different lives
Wasn't it too much,
It would be for most people
But then you aren't most people.

You were unique.
Like no one before or after.
A proletariat hero and a materialist.
A patriot and a father, a husband and a pioneer
Now what else is there?
I guess you weren't Dr. Ehrlich or Louis Pasteur
But maybe they weren't you.

Mama just said "SPRING IS COMING"
EVERYTHING IS AWAKENING BUT DADDY
I THOUGHT I WOULD DIE.
Isn't it terrible that, with all my education, I can believe nothing
I only believed in you. You were my religion and my teacher and
My belief in human nature. What do I believe now?
That the other side is better!
You told me a thousand times that there is no heaven or hell.

I loved our nights at the beach when I was a little girl.
How you told me stories about the miracle of the ocean
The world you showed me was full of miracles and we
We were only a small part of it
Remember at camp when they told you what a poor camper I
  was
That I never made my bed or did K.P. like the others
That I didn't seem to want to be a kibbutznik and, after all,
You built the camp. Remember the embarrassment.
You called me and said . . "IT'S OK BABY. YOU DON'T HAVE TO
  BE
ANYTHING YOU DON'T WANT TO BE. YOU CAN STAY OR
  COME HOME.
OR WE'LL COME AND GET YOU.
MAYBE IT'S NOT FOR YOU"
And I was so relieved.
You always thought I was OK even in your embarrassment.
Here you were, devoting time, energy and love to something
Your own daughter didn't want.
Always OK
Nobody ever had that. No one I know.

Remember when we had to ask for some shillings in
The airport on our way back to the States because I had spent
Every cent and it was Sunday and all the check cashing places
Were closed.
How mad you were at me.
But only for an instant.
I could do no wrong.
I did so many, didn't I, Daddy?
So many things that another parent would have—well, I didn't

Know any other father but you, so I don't know how they would
    have
Handled them.
But in your way you let me know. Well, it's only that "you're
An artist. Artists aren't like real people." So many excuses for me.
You used to say my kitchens were Korea
You would pop in and, in an instant, get it all together so it
Would look like I had done it. A big man like you cleaning
A kitchen. You would say "GET OUT OF HERE, BABY, IT WILL
    TAKE
ME A MINUTE."
No one could believe our feeling one for each other.
MY BIG SHERMAN TANK WAS ALWAYS THERE
WHERE IS THAT TANK, NOW, DADDY?

I HAVE ALWAYS MADE MY OWN RULES FOR MYSELF AS YOU
    TAUGHT ME.
I HAVE ALWAYS BELIEVED AT THE VERY BOTTOM OF MY
    SOUL
THAT I WAS BLESSED WITH THOSE SPECIAL GIFTS THAT
    EITHER
GOD OR NATURE OR THE GENETIC STRUCTURE PUT TO-
    GETHER WITH ME IN MIND
IN A DIFFERENT WAY
THAT I WAS SPECIAL
ABLE TO LIVE LIFE FULLER AND BETTER AND LONGER
THAT I HAD THE STRENGTH THAT YOUR AND MOTHER'S
    SPECIAL LOVE
PUMPED INTO ME SO I COULD SURVIVE
THAT IS YOUR LEGACY
THAT IS WHAT YOU REALLY GAVE ME.
THE ABILITY TO SURVIVE
I did have you for a time others would say was
LONG
Not long enough.
Could it, Daddy?
Never enough time.
This is the longest time I haven't seen you since I went away
To school
Remember that first goodbye at Dearborn Station in Chicago.
But this one is the long goodbye, isn't it?
It is hard to believe that but yet I must.
I remember that Joseph Schildkraut when I was his student used
    to

Say that you were the actor in the family.
That you were indeed the star.
That it was you who should be on the stage not me.
That I was pale next to you
I still am.
You are not yet a thought in my mind's eye
You are in front of me alive, well, smiling and so
Filled with life.
The feel of your energy is still upon me as it was yesterday
But I am cold
The chill is in my back and under my eyes
My fantasy tells me that your person is here
My truth knows you are not
I want so to lie to myself
I always could before
But not now
This truth is too strong
It has snapped me out of my fantasy as nothing else
It has made me look at a world without you
It is unbearable and yet I will bear
It is the rite of passage
The time to end the story
I will never let go,
That you must know
I will never let you rest in a peaceful place
I wonder if you could see me now . . . how I yearn to thank you
If you could know that your not being here will make us all
Forever cold.
I who believe nothing know that you will live on with me
For all my days. Not only to remember
But to help me make it till tomorrow.
And I am going to try.

But it is so terribly hard, Daddy.
Harder than anything you ever made me do
I'm not so sure that I'm going to pass this particular lesson
Not sure at all.

People always talked about your big giant desk. It was a desk for
A cardinal not a person. Were you a cardinal too?
And on the wall there was this huge picture of me . . six of them I
Remember and you used to say that "IF ORSON WELLES COULD
    DO IT IN *CITIZEN KANE,* WHY NOT SOL?"
It was really funny, but you figured maybe someone will see it
And put me in the movies. And it was seen and I was in the
    movies
I don't know how really glad you were of it, and the funny
Part of your office was that you had a big safe visibly in sight and
Since you didn't remember numbers you had the combination
    pasted
On the door. In case someone came in to rob you, they could get
At it easily. Now who would do that? Really.

I remember when you were offered all kinds of money for the
Desk and you said "No, it's my daughter's . . not for sale"
Now the desk sits in my living room, the chair behind it empty.
And up above that is your father's picture . . he lived to be
    ninety-
Seven, Couldn't you have done that?
I expected at least that.
There was a romance in that office. It was as imposing as you
    were
And rather out of sync with a furniture store. It looked like it
Belonged at MGM, it probably did.
You wore a doubled-breasted suit and a huge black coat with a
    big

Cigar, it always looked like you were head of some foreign
Opera company. I thought there was a lot of Sol Hurok in you
So did you.
But it was the Jewish theatre that you kept alive and it wasn't too
Successful, was it?
Well, then I guess you weren't Sol Hurok
So what difference did a last name mean.

When I was in the theatre in New York, how you loved the Stage
Delicatessen . . . I think it was because you could talk all night
To theatre people . . . then we loved the Russian Tea Room be-
    cause you
Could converse with the waiters in Russian and if it was late we
Stayed to hear any music that was being played by somebody
    with
A mandolin or a balalaika or just a capella
You hated the Communists, because they were unfair to your
    Jews
But you loved the romance that once was Russia and you adored
Gorky and Tolstoy and Dostoyevsky. You took me to *Crime and
Punishment* performed in Russian when I was eleven in a theatre
In New York. I don't know why, but I think you loved SHOLEM
    ALEICHEM
Best. You saw it so many times with me and with the children—
    you
Just adored Zero as we all did. He's gone too. You can't swap
Stories unless he's where you are. THERE AREN'T ANY MORE
    FIDDLERS
ON THE ROOF IN ANATEVKA.
It is a world all gone away. A world of charm and noise and
Intellect—no, Daddy, you didn't go to school like Harvard but
    what
You have taught. My God.

You were the best date and the most fun ever. All of my sexy
Girlfriends always wanted to go along with us when I was in
    New York,
Remember? I would say yes . . he's my real father . . honest
And they wouldn't believe me. It was such fun.
You worried about my crazy diets and my New York colds.
But you let me do it because I wanted to.
That's what I'm going to miss, the fun. The fun was terrific.
You just had it Daddy. Sure a lot of girls' daddies can't take
Them to the theatre but the love of a daddy to a little girl or even
A bigger girl makes her whole life different.
I don't know why more women don't know.
I don't know why they don't keep the daddies around

Maybe you are watching your
Friends play pinochle and kibitzing somewhere, all drinking
Tea with a lump of sugar and talking great thoughts.
I can't bear that place, so maybe I will dream up something spe-
    cial as
You would for me. Something different.
Right now, I don't know what it could be. If I could believe that
You were at a big dinner with Zionists raising money or in
    Solomon's
Bookshop on Fairfax or in a delicatessen, then it wouldn't be so
    bad
But I don't know where you are
I saw where they put you and I hate it

But that is reality and didn't you tell me to always push it away
   if
It hurts me.
WELL, IT DOES.
AND I CAN'T PUSH IT AWAY.

The day we put you in that ugly place I told my husband to take
Little Lisa Beth who is so like me to the best store here and
To buy her the prettiest navy blue coat they had. The very best.
So that she wouldn't think that because the body of Grandpa
Was not around things would be different.
HE BOUGHT THE COAT.
THEY ARE DIFFERENT.
It will never even be remotely like you
She will know the love of a father. He adores her and
Always says that she's perfect . . . but you. She will not have
Known you long enough.
Today is forever.
And it's an awful day, just awful.
You know what you would say.
"Now, listen, you go in and wash your face and I'll take you to the
Very biggest dinner in America."
Lots of good people will buy me anything,
But they are not you.
Remember from *Can-Can*
And Cole Porter
"IT'S THE WRONG TIME
AND THE WRONG PLACE
THOUGH YOUR FACE IS CHARMING, IT'S THE WRONG
    FACE . . ."
IT'S NOT YOUR FACE . . DADDY IT'S NOT YOUR FACE.
AND IT'S NOT ALL RIGHT WITH ME.

Of all of us, Mama has lost the most
I don't know how she will find a way to live

Or even if she will
She has such class
She does not want to leave your house even for a minute
She wants not to change one moment of your atmosphere
This morning she told me that when her brother was killed her
     father
Told her his life was a debt he had to pay to God
And she said that your end was a debt that we had to pay to
     nature!
No wonder, Daddy, that you always told me what a great lady
     Mama was
Everything she says now, as always, has not a moment of the
     common
Wail of women who lose their husbands. She talks in epic terms
As if it were being spoken by Aristotle
It is unbelievable, her grief.
And yet that tiny figure does not want any comfort.
She wants her aloneness to be closer to you.
You always told me that we know what people are when they
     are
In stress. My God, she is something. A broken figure, but not
Wanting me to hear her heart. This morning she asked me if I'd
Eaten breakfast. Can you believe that Daddy? Can you? In the
Midst of her pain, she is thinking I should eat.
No wonder your eyes never strayed and, in the hospital, when she
     told
You she wouldn't be able to go to Israel any more . . she told

Me you said you would carry her. Oh Daddy, such love you had
   one
For the other. People thought that maybe you didn't because of
   all
The time you spend with me. Daddy people know nothing. She
   had
To be who she is or you wouldn't have been who you were. Why
   do
I come to the knowing of that so late?
Or did I know it all along, Daddy?
Did I?
I must have, but I was too silly to admit it.

If you have gone to a special place I wonder if it is in the
Same heaven as Ben Gurion and Zero Mostel and your Beloved
   Sholem
Aleichem and Rabbi Nussbaum and Muni Weisenfreund, and
   Maurice
Schwartz. I wonder if there is a special place for just a certain
Kind of people . . maybe not all famous. But special in their own
   way
Then it wouldn't be so bad.
Did I tell you that this year I will not have Pesach. I just can't
You have to forgive me that, I just wouldn't be able to do it.
I'm so glad you saw Shepsie's Bar Mitzvah, and I have all of those
Pictures. He is so beautiful, Daddy, and so gentle.
If you are in that special rarefied place maybe you are all

Talking big things or reading *KING LEAR* in Yiddish, wouldn't
    that
Be a marvelous idea?
I'm trying to think of all the great places where you may have
Gone instead of places where I don't want to think you are.

Remember the Louvre in Paris.
You stood me next to the *Mona Lisa* and tried to photograph me
Until the policeman took away the camera
You loved things lush but you always remembered where you
Had come from and what you really were
A boy who cut away his past and tucked his religion under his
coat
And went out to forge a world and feed an ever growing inter-
related
Family.
Someone dear just told me that soon I will forget the pain
And remember only the love
It's hard for me to believe that day will ever come
But let it come already . . doesn't that sound like you?
But today the pain still sits on my chest.
And makes going out into the world seem unimportant
The days go by without my energy to see them through
Without a noise to hear you going up the steps
Without you
BUT I WILL NEVER BE WITHOUT YOU, DADDY.
BECAUSE I AM YOU.

I remember how you held court in my living room day by day
With girlfriends . . . everyone always wanted to
Talk to you about marriages, and whether or not they should get
Divorces . . and it was a social thing.
It was only lately, you not feeling as super as usual, that
Part was curtailed, but you were certainly in demand.
They ask me now do I ever think I'll really see you again and
It is too soon to answer
I only know that I don't stop seeing you.
I cannot really believe these past weeks.
It is a black cloud inside and outside of me that just seemingly
Won't change color.
The big chair in the room looks like it lost a friend
If I just asked it
I look into the sky to see if I see your smile on a cloud
And I can't find it.
You didn't tutor me too well in what to think when you weren't
Around, did you!

I don't think I'll ever be warm again, ever. I remember how you
Used to rub your big hand on top of my back in New York in the
    dead
Of winter and I would think that I had been touched by a
    heating
Pad. It wasn't your hand, it was your love.
It took away all of the cold.
Nobody's hand is that big. No.
Nor will anyone know the approximate moment to rub my back.

That's it, always there, backstage, front, on top, in between.
SO, AS NO ONE WOULD NOTICE OR EVERYONE WOULD
   NOTICE,
THERE FOR EVERY NEED AND EVERY JOB.
YOU WERE THERE.

Little Lisa Beth tries so hard to comfort me
Last night in the middle of whatever she kisses me with her
Soft baby cheeks then busies herself with her dolls or her books
She is so good with all of her things, as if each of those toy
Fantasies were her children. She is pure enchantment, but she
Misses you and talks about her Babar with such love.
You were Babar the elephant in the green suit. (Like Peter
    Ustinov)
Daddy, such joy you brought us all.
Forgetting nothing.
Last night, Shepsie was talking about the blackout in New York
When he didn't want to call you so you wouldn't panic and he
Called Grandma Jeannette to tell her he was all right and you
    and Mom
Got the information softened
Then his eyes got watery.
It's as if you're sitting next to us.
Watching us and hearing what we are saying.
The news from Israel is terrible this morning.
Will they never find Peace until they are all dead.
And this time it was children.
Daddy, you see there aren't any heads there, it seems.

I wanted you not to miss Lisa Beth's growing into womanhood.
So I am going to spoil her as you did me
And deny her only that which would cause her pain
So that, as she grows, you'll know she'll be in beautiful coats
With white gloves and navy blue dresses and long hair and no

Earrings, even though fashion dictates it.
She will be brought up as closely as I remember so she
Will have the knowledge that she is wonderful because I am not
Going to tell her, but show her, and I will make her know how
Special she is.
It won't be you, but it will be close.

You always told your children and grandchildren about the
    miracles.
Those special biblical miracles like Chanukah and Moses parting
The waters and the Burning Bush and the miracle of tiny
Israel that stays despite its enemies
But why couldn't you have been the miracle? To beat God's call.
The one I wanted
To make the days pass in any kind of joy
WHY COULDN'T GOD GRANT THAT MIRACLE IN *FIDDLER*
    THAT ZERO
SANG SO MANY TIMES?
Oh Daddy, I will never stop asking myself those questions that I
Indeed cannot answer.
It just didn't come.
Maybe it was the wrong time of the year for miracles.
But as the night is coming
And I am trying hard to be a person
The tears not running down my face
But backed up under my eyes.
Oh, Daddy, Daddy
Where are you?

I was blessed, you said, with beauty, brains, guts and the ability
To survive and land on my feet . . friends call it chutzpah and
　　magic
But I call it you
I was blessed with you and, after that, it didn't almost matter
　　what
God left out or what was cosmetically put in
But without you
I got unblessed
My eyes are a muddy blue
My face parched with tears which I know are indelibly stained on
My paleness and my mouth has a dry quiver
Daddy, will I ever look like your girl again
I doubt it
For everyone else I'll be OK
Everyone is not you
If you saw me now you would say
FOR THEM YOU LOOK ALL RIGHT BUT NOT FOR ME
WHERE IS THE SHINE ON MY ORANGE?

Remember when I was so sick and there was real danger, and all
The food the doctors gave made me vomit and you stayed in the
Hospital all thirty-one days, never going to your office
Until you brought me a corned beef sandwich on rye and I ate it
And suddenly I got better and the next day I was on my way
    home.
Why couldn't I have found a way, Daddy?
What didn't I feed you?
Why did I let the doctors take care of you?
Why did I trust them?
How will I know if I did everything I could have?
How will my guilt ever leave me alone
Or is it supposed to stay
Don't worry, it stays anyway.

This morning because the air was so crisp and the sun shining and

My house so quiet, I was thinking of the awnings when spring comes

Outside Bonwit Teller in New York.

How you loved the color violet, you bought me violets too.

Not for the same reasons as my yellow rose but you even had the

Joy in your eye to notice that.

You noticed everything.

I USED TO SAY THAT YOU SAW TOO MUCH.

YOU USED TO ANSWER THAT THERE WAS NEVER ENOUGH TO SEE.

IT WAS THE POETRY IN YOUR SOUL

YOU ALWAYS SAID IT WAS FROM YOUR MOTHER'S SIDE OF THE FAMILY

BUT I THOUGHT IT WAS A SPECIAL SAGE MATERIAL THAT HAD BEEN GIVEN TO

YOU ALONE THROUGH SOME OSMOSIS.

Everything that gave life spice and energy was part of you.

Each day if there wasn't a tragedy in Europe and if the store

Went OK, there was something special about it

Remember, how you used to take me out of school for a whole day just

To have an adventure. I do that too, Daddy, all the time.

I can't do it as much with my son now because he is so busy

With his being

But I do it with my daughter.

YOU COULD NEVER BELIEVE THAT AMERICA COULD HAVE
    ALLOWED SIX MILLION JEWS TO DIE, NEVER.
EVEN IN YOUR MUDDLEDNESS, THE LAST NIGHT OF YOUR
    LIFE, YOU SCREAMED
"UNITED STATES OF AMERICA . . WHY DIDN'T YOU STOP
    HIM?"
YOU SAID IT CLEAR AS A CRY FROM A BROKEN ANIMAL
YOUR SPIRIT WAS BROKEN THAT NIGHT, DADDY, BUT YOUR
    HEAD SAID
EXACTLY WHAT WAS IN YOUR HEART, TO YOUR LAST
    BREATH.
WHY, DADDY, WHY?
WHY, THIS LAST MOMENT, WERE YOU STILL THINKING OF A
    HOLOCAUST THAT
BIGGER MEN THAN YOU TRIED TO STOP AND COULDN'T?
MEN WITH MORE INFLUENCE COULD NOT STOP THE TER-
    RORISM WHICH IS
STILL THIS MORNING'S HEADLINE
I SHOULD DO SOMETHING DADDY
WITH THIS ENERGY THAT YOU LEFT ME
NOT ONLY THIS BOOK BUT SOMETHING INTERNATIONAL TO
    PUT YOUR STAMP
ON IT.
I THINK YOU WOULD WANT THAT.
I DON'T KNOW HOW AT THE MOMENT, BUT IT WILL COME
    TO ME IN THESE
NEXT DAYS WHEN I TRY TO HEAL MY OWN HEART, IN DOING
WHAT YOU WOULD WANT.
GOD, I LOVE YOU, DADDY.

You told me in such a way every night on the phone, no matter
    how much
We had argued. I will do something, Daddy,
I will.
It's just this moment it is tough to know how to make it for the
Next hour. But I will.

I can't let your death go unnoticed except by just well-wishers
And openhearted people.
No, I must do something in your name so you can be proud to say
Wherever you are, she didn't just sit and cry . . . LOOK AT HER
THAT'S MY DAUGHTER.

I have been in the greatest mourning but I just realized
And through this writing have found out that I am mourning
Our life more than your death
How stupid of me not to have known all these past days.
Known that maybe the Irish are right . . . when someone they
    love
Goes away, they celebrate, but, then, I'm not Irish and I have
Never been to a wake, never. But I have held here my own
Special kind. Temples seem all wrong for my feelings. No matter
What you told me about the great teachers and how I needed to
Learn from them! Learning from you was enough. It was all I
Needed ever.

I need you to know that everything I have known and loved and
    been
A part of has you in it.
When I look in the mirror, I know how you would want me to
    look
If you were here.
How you would want me to stay the clock, and
That I am afraid I cannot do
The days will go by
And I will try to love without your presence as best as I can
I will tell stories about you
And I will know that I was adored for exactly what I was
Then and now,
As the seasons change and as I grow old
I will have known someone very rare
A good and great man with a humor which will have to keep me
    on
The days which will seem unbearable.
Because I won't hear that special laugh which could always
    make
My spirit soar.

I HAVE HAD SOMETHING
A TOTAL UNSELFISH LOVE
THE KIND THAT ONLY A SPECIAL PARENT CAN GIVE AND A
    CHILD CAN
HOLD ALL OF HER LIFE
FROM A MAN
AND THAT MAN JUST HAPPENS TO HAVE BEEN MY FATHER

I am asked a thousand times
"How are you?"
I either shrug or say something the asker wants to hear
I am not fine
I was fine because you made me think so
And my courage wanes from time to time
I cannot believe the rest of my life without you
I can't imagine how the years will be or even the days
It is inconceivable
I cannot know who I can truly bother with madness
I will have to either stop having it
Or find someone new
Both impossible!!
I can imagine my son growing and finding his nest
I can even imagine with difficulty my daughter going off
But you
That is so unfathomable to me,
And the only time I can communicate with you is when I sit here
Writing to you.
Maybe I'll do that forever or until I am so old that the keys
No longer work as I punch them.
Daddy the whole thing seems impossible, but it is true
Terribly true.
My whole person reminds me. The phone that never rings
Your voice that doesn't boom up the steps
and that sound, "BABY"
That sound that at once angered and pleased me.
JUST FOR ONE MINUTE TELL ME HOW TO DO MY DAYS

TELL ME WHAT WOULD PLEASE YOU, REALLY
COME BACK AS IN *OUR TOWN* AND LOOK AT ME JUST ONCE
REMEMBER IN *CAROUSEL* BILLY BIGELOW DID THAT.
HE WOULD TELL ME
ISN'T THERE ANYONE UP THERE THAT KNOWS ANYTHING
SURELY THEY MUST KNOW
THAT IS THEIR BUSINESS
PLEASE DADDY, LOOK AT ME ONE MORE TIME AND LET ME
 HEAR
"BABY."

Thiirty Days

A month it is today
I still sit alone as much as I can
The very heart of me really gone out.
I dress everyday and clean and comb but my pretty clothes sit
     idly
In their closet their bodies in cellophane and I wear clean clothes
But nothing super
I still am in mourning even though Jews can be out of
Mourning
In 30 days
I really don't know when I will be whole again
I stopped talking and got quiet
Can you imagine me quiet
Can you
Without any bounce
You used to say I bounced down the streets when I walked
Not now anymore
I hardly move
I am comfortable here because I am close to you here for some
     reason   .
I want only to write to you
To tell you things
About my appointments and what is happening or not.
I need that.

Without you I tell others
But it has lost its magic .. all of it
Remember the little black suit that we used to fold up for in-
    terviews
Remember all of that
How can I possibly forget anything and go on as if the world
  were the
Same for me it just is not.
It doesn't have any of your smile in it
And I can't manufacture it.
I really really can't
Not any of it.
For the very first time in my life I feel poor.
Something you would hate but I do feel terribly poor.

The sun is shining today and the children are at their children's
Things I don't expect them to stop their brand of living because I
Have
I don't expect anything
Only that someway someday I'll get some more orders from you
    on how
I should conduct myself and do my things.
I can't seem to get that
Maybe if I go to a different place
Maybe then I'll hear those sounds.
That's the sadness
Not to hear you
It stifles my life and destroys my soul.

It really isn't whether it is right or wrong.
It just is.
That's all.
Just is.

Forever

The days are passing yes
But without your pulse to give their time its energy
I find more and more that I am alone
Not for want of people
But of my own desire
No one has known what I have had
And I wish not to explain it to strangers
I have become silent
Not wanting to share our life with even our children
They are tired of my mourning
I went out today and saw a bottle of Dry Sack and bought it ..
A reminder of you
And strawberries, hard apples, rye bread .. all a reminder a
    pain and
A cut
All of it is you was you and a thousand reminders all of my days.
How will I find a tomorrow without you
The nights are terrible
The pills help but not enough
The children try. Only my children and husband and Mama
I care for no one else and nothing
I am bitter and I hate the spring when you loved me so in
Your navy blue
When you looked at me and said your eyes are a spring day
No one will look at me that way again because I am not that girl

Anymore
I am not a girl
I am a saddened woman
Bereft of love and fantasy
Living in the real world.
The real world isn't anything
It just isn't
Not without you in it
Without you it is a bore.
A dreadful horrible nowhere place.
Is the place where you are better, Daddy?

The ammunition of some kind of glossy faith would have helped
It was the reality of Hitler which took it away from us wasn't it
I remember Grandpa used to talk about a Messiah
And you used to scream, where is he?
And Grandpa would say that he would come
And as Jews were slaughtered and the numbers grew
You became less a believer
And that is why now I don't know where to think you are
Though I prayed on those days
The days I heard that I was supposed to
I never really prayed
BECAUSE YOU SAID THE HOLOCAUST WAS NOT STOPPING
    BECAUSE OF
A MESSIAH BUT BECAUSE OF AMERICAN GUNS
SO MUCH REALITY FOR A TINY GIRL
SO MUCH DAMNATION
AND YET YOU HAD ME BELIEVE IN MYSELF
IN MY OWN POWER
AND IN MY OWN WILL
YOU HAD ME DO ALL THAT AND LIVE THESE YEARS AND
    BEAR CHILDREN
AND ACTUALLY BELIEVE NOTHING.
I wonder if it was fair
Wouldn't it have been simpler for me now
Rather than sitting here confused and frightened because I
Have no answers even to myself.
But, then, does anyone
Yesterday someone told me that Aristotle didn't know either
That gave me comfort only for a moment.

When I go to the cavern where your name is written it seems
As if you don't belong there. It is a man-made place
For men like you with the things it is supposed to have
I would have put you in a place more familiar to all of us
But the law says no . .
Whose law
But no matter
That is done
It is all done
The only thing I can cheat from death are my memories
These no one can take.
Until I too am gone . .
You did believe in luck though
And feel . . you did a lot with that
But God's . . No, I'm afraid you didn't.
I used to hear you say, "THE SINS OF THE FATHERS"
AND YOUR MORALITY WAS A BOY'S FROM A CHASID
YOUR INNER BEING I THINK WAS A DISBELIEVER

It is so lucky I still have a little girl who needs me
That is my luck
She is so like me
Her sentiment is unbelievable
But you knew that
I am sure. You said it often enough
My son is so big, bigger and more manly by the minute
But she is just wonderful
Brave and frightened
She will be happier if she is not like me—but she is!
Life's pain won't throw her if she is like the others
But how do I do it.
Then too its joys won't be there, will they?
Remember Grandma used to say that you must know pain so
    that joy
Is sweeter
Now is the worst pain I have ever known because you were my
    best joy
If you hadn't been splendid . . . that's a word for you, splendid . . .
I remember
Splendid . . .
Oh Daddy.

Messages

I look at the pictures that Mother brought last night and as usual
I was in a haze of tears.
How incredibly handsome you two were
What a dreadful thing age is
But if not age then early death and both are dreadful.
Age seems to be the beginning of death
But why did it take till now for me to understand?
It is because I have never faced the thought of my own?
Not until now
Now I am facing life without what I want most.
A million years of loneliness—is that to be my pogram?
Is that what I have to look forward to?
Emptiness which began again in the night when I walked alone
Until I woke my little child to beg her to have a cookie
Any excuse to try and push away this loneliness.
There is so much for me to do
And yet I can do nothing

Today was the worst . . .
It was one long dreary disappointment of life
And no liquor in the house to soothe the pain
The liquor neither soothes nor
Eliminates anything
It only dulls for a moment the forever pain which is never
    soothed.
I cannot believe I will ever again walk as if the world belonged to
Me
I can never ever again believe that I will know real joy
How will it happen that I will live again?
If it were up to me
And I had that choice I would choose to crawl away in some
    deep
Shell forever knowing I would be warm and protected
Why do I need to seek that which makes me sad
Did I not forego that long ago
I find myself again in a world to compete
When I choose not to do that anymore
I choose to make my own world.
To live my passions as I please
And to watch two beautiful new lives unfold
So maybe my joy won't be gone forever
And I will find at least a place from which not to hide
But to walk into the sun and watch my blossoms unfold
It is time for me to have that joy.
To be a mother again
And not to compete with those who search for that eternal star

To give them joy
No, I have decided I will walk again
But with a new gait.
I have known loss and see love in the eyes of my children
And in both there is life.

You honestly made us all believe that you were a lion
Strong and hard and that nothing life could throw at you could
    hurt you

  What fools we were not to know you were as human and frail
  As all of us, but we didn't want to believe that
  You were the big star in the family and all of us shone
  Under you
  By ourselves we were just simple mortals without your
    elegance
  To make us shine clearer
  We are a company without a star
  Didn't you know that was impossible
  We can't even begin life's play without a star
  And I can't find anything in any of us which even gets close
  To you

We are without our shepherd
A floundering flock
If you hadn't made yourself the star maybe we could have
Survived this as other people do every day and go on badly but go
On
But you were so all encompassing that we flounder and are
    fearful
And look for something we know not to take us away from our
    pain.
And yet as the sun is shining down through my windows at this
    moment
I cannot feel its heat, only my pain that never goes away.

I am a different person now
It is so evident
Everyone says so
I almost never smile
Wouldn't you have hated that
I am going to try
I decided this morning
Really try to be what you would want me to be if you
Could direct me
I WILL BE YOUR DAUGHTER, ABLE TO TAKE THIS TER-
    RIBLE THRUST
THAT LIFE HAS GIVEN ME
BUT IT IS GOING TO BE VERY VERY HARD, BECAUSE I AM
    NOT GOING
TO HEAR YOU SHOUT, BRAVO
NO ONE WILL BE APPLAUDING IN THE WINGS
AND, AS MY FAMILY AND FRIENDS SAY, I MUST DO IT FOR
MYSELF
I DON'T KNOW WHO MYSELF IS BUT I AM GOING TO DO
    MY DAMNDEST
TO TRY
To try until I can bury this pain underneath so far it is
Never seen by strangers and seldom by friends.

I think the only way to function is to find other things to scream
About . . . have fights with . . . win or lose those little battles.
I won't be good for anybody this way. Maybe Camus was right.
    Maybe
We should live for today because death hangs over us all the time.
But we don't think of that.
I always thought you would never die or not until you were so
    old I
Would beg God to take you
But you see how wrong I was
Had I known, we could have had a brilliant week before . . like
    the men who
Know that they are going to die, . . then we would have played
    as before
But we did talk for hours before you got sick . . . three hours on
    the
Phone . . but we could have had bagels and wine and chocolate
    mousse . . .
Remember how the man brought the mousse at Les Am-
    bassadeurs in Paris
So French. And he turned out to be a Jewish student. Oh, Daddy,
Such fun . . so many memories to fill my head until the day I
    die . . of
Joy and not of pain.

YOU ARE MY MEMORY OF JOY
YOU BIGGER THAN LIFE, IN WHATEVER THEY CALL THIS
    DEATH BUSINESS
YOU STAY THE STAR OF THE SHOW
THE BIG DREAMER
THE DOER
THE MAN
And I told Mama tonight that she picked the right one for me . .
How smart of that lady.
A blind man doesn't know he is blind if he has never seen
But he does know if he has ever seen the colors and the light.
You had every color, Daddy, every light
And though I will live . . .
I must . . .
I will live like a man who has seen everything and now has been
    blinded
Because I had seen all of your colors.
You taught me all you knew and made me believe in myself.
I won't even try to fill my loneliness.
That is for me alone.
But I have hope, Daddy
I will give some of you to my children and they will give some of
    you
To theirs and you will live on as part of all of us.
A rare and special present the young girl said.
How lucky, said the writer who writes so eloquently
And I say, good night, Daddy
Tonight I may not sleep as I would have but I think
Maybe I will find a peace I have not known before
I WILL KNOW THROUGH THIS LETTER TO YOU THAT I HAVE
    HAD THAT PERFECT
LOVE

FROM A FATHER TO A DAUGHTER WHICH I WILL IN SOME
    WAY BE ABLE TO GIVE
TO OTHERS WHO BELIEVE IN NOTHING AS I DO BUT WERE
    SOMEHOW GIVEN THE
PRESENT OF BELIEVING IN THEMSELVES.
MAYBE YOU HELPED THEM TO BELIEVE THAT.
THEN YOUR LIFE WAS INDEED NOT WASTED
NOT ONE MINUTE
IT HAD ALL OF THE COLOR AND JOY AND HOPE AND PAIN
    AND LOVE THAT IT
WAS SUPPOSED TO HAVE
BUT I HAD YOU AND THAT IS THE BEST OF ALL POSSIBLE
    WORLDS.
GOODNIGHT, DADDY.

Big Sol

This morning the sun shone and I put my face together as best I
Could and suddenly decided that I was to pick up my pieces and
Stop weeping at every moment, but continuing loving you, I am
Going to put this broken family together.
As you would have said, ENOUGH ALREADY
It will never be enough because you were too much
But damn it I am going to try.
I threw away the pills that dulled my senses
And have started planning my tomorrows.
I HAVE HAD A TERRIBLE ACCIDENT.
I WILL NEED A LONG TIME TO RECUPERATE
AFTER ALL AREN'T I SOL'S DAUGHTER
AND THE BILLING IS STILL TERRIFIC.

I HAVE A GNAWING TERRIBLE EMPTY SPACE
IF THERE IS A GOD HE KNOWS THAT EVERYONE AROUND ME
     HAS REALLY I MEAN REALLY
TRIED TO FILL IT
IT DOESN'T GET BETTER
IT GETS DIFFERENT
I FUNCTION
I HAVE TO
BUT I AM NOT THE SAME
MY HUMOR ISN'T AT ALL WHAT IT WAS
MY LOOKS . . WELL I STARTED OUT WITH A TERRIFIC SET

BUT IF YOU LOOK CLOSE
UNDER THE EYES THERE ARE TERRIBLE FOREVER WET
    MARKS.
I DON'T WANT TO GET OVER MISSING YOU
THE PSYCHIATRIST IS AN ASS
EVERYONE IS
THEY KNOW NOTHING
I NOTICE MY SON KEEPS TELLING ME HE FILLS HIS LIFE SO
    FULL HE CAN'T GRIEVE
SO DO I
BULLSHIT
I GRIEVE
BUT NOT FOR MY FATHER
NO NOT THAT
FOR THE ONE PERSON IN THE WHOLE GOD DAMN WORLD
    THAT THOUGHT I WAS
BETTER THAN I WAS
MY EGO NEEDS YOU SO BAD . .
BUT THE DAYS PASS WITHOUT YOU
THE SUN COMES UP IN THE MORNING AND I PLAN MY
    TOMORROW
AS IF YOU WERE HERE
BUT THE EMPTINESS THAT I FELT THE DAY THEY TOOK YOU
THAT HAS NOT BEEN FILLED
JUST YESTERDAY I WANTED TO CALL YOU AND TELL YOU
    THINGS

BUT YOU WEREN'T THERE
I PUT DOWN THE PHONE.
DID I LEARN TO BELIEVE THAT YOU WEREN'T COMING BACK
I DID NOT.
I LEARNED TO BELIEVE THAT YOU WERE SO MUCH A PART
    OF MY PERSON THAT I
WILL
I WILL LIVE MY LIFE BUT NOT ALL INTACT.
I CAN'T FAKE THAT.
I AM INJURED
A PART OF ME GONE
THE VERY BOTTOM OF MY INTESTINES BRUISED AND
    MAIMED
I AM SUCH A GREAT CON ARTIST THAT THOSE AROUND ME
    BELIEVE I AM OK
I AM A MINUTE EVERY MINUTE FROM SCREAMING.
MY ANGER SITS INSIDE ME LIKE A FESTERING BOIL. MORE
    AND MORE I KNOW
IN THE SMALLEST OF MOMENTS
AND FOR THE SILLIEST THINGS HOW BADLY I NEED YOU
AND YET THERE IS NO CURE FOR ME
EXCEPT MAYBE LITTLE LISA BETH
SHE TELLS ME THAT YOU SEE US
THAT YOU WATCH US AND THAT YOU KNOW EVERYTHING,

MAYBE SHE IS RIGHT
DAMN I HOPE SO.
DIDN'T YOU ALWAYS SAY NEVER TO BE SO TALL THAT YOU
    CAN'T BEND DOWN TO A SMALL CHILD.
DIDN'T YOU SAY THAT DADDY.
I LISTEN
I LISTEN VERY HARD.
I BEND ALL THE WAY DOWN
AND I TRY
I TRY VERY HARD TO HEAR.

Spring

The leaves are so green outside my window
The sun playing its special games to make them appear in many
    colors
The sky the bluest of blue clear and elegant
And the white, gray and green clouds signifying that a new sea-
    son is
Beginning
The long winter is over
The rains have finally disappeared
We will have a green spring
But it won't be our spring Daddy
It will be the whole world's but not ours.
You will sleep through this spring
And never see another unless in those special places where you
    are, they
Have it greener
It won't be green for me it will be as gray as it was
I won't even see it
Any of it
My eyes too scarred to see or care
Without you it will be cold
The winter having remained
To ever remind me
That you alone
The best person to walk with

At this very time
Are no more.
It . . . . . it will be a cold and unhappy spring
It is darkest winter all over again.

So many I love are gone
So much I adore is no longer
I look inside to remember and find nothing
None of the joy of life is inside my soul
What a despicable thought
Only my children
So beautiful
And is not my husband a saint
To have to bear me as I am now
My dear mother patient and shy
Alone
She is forever alone
Without any solace
Bereft of joy
Longing for that kind of love that can only be shared by two
Whose lives have really intertwined
Should I not glory in my own life
And the gifts that I have been given
Is it then not possible for me to find some sunshine
In this darkened part of my heart that no one hears
And I feel so deeply
There must be a way for this longing to find its final rest

There must be something that my dear daddy has left to me that
    was ours alone
That I can communicate to him which would give him joy in
    that faraway
Place he now calls home.
Is there a way to end this vigil I seem to need.
It will end when it ends.
But it never will.
It will be ever with me
I want to talk to you Daddy.
I want to ask you things.
Silly things that only an only daughter feels
And thinks and wants to hear again
I thought you would always find a way to let me hear you.
And I sit motionless waiting for the sound.
The intrusion in my life that was so necessary for my days.
Daddy, Daddy—did I hear you?

Right at this moment I feel my loss terribly.
I have no one to tell anything to
No one to share the excitement of the phone calls or the fact that
What I've written about you could be a play or a book or a movie.
No one though I have my husband and my dear children
None of them are you and the loneliness is the worst part.
I don't think I can bear any of that.
No one to really share the very bottom of my soul with anymore
I am so sorry for myself it is unbelievable.
My pain does not get better with the days
It just gets plainer that I am lonelier
For the thing that I need
I wonder if everyone alive who loves, loves like this
I wonder but it doesn't matter
I have and I am alive and alone with only my memories
Of that radiance inside of me
Daddy why did you go away and leave me
Why aren't you still a part of my every day
I would take the smallest part
A minute a day for the rest of my life.
Oh how selfish I am
That I would want you any way I could, even if you were not all
    there, just
To have any of you . . that would be marvelous
But now I have nothing to keep desire inside of me
Nothing.

I have begun to hate the days
I have not loved anything this month
Really
And that is the worst of it
Not to love or want anything
Daddy where are you

It's close to Easter time . .
Remember when I was a little girl you brought home a rabbit
And Mama screamed that it was an injustice to the poor thing.
And I cried so bitterly that we kept it and built it a home with
Carpeting so that it wouldn't get arthritis, and finally when
    spring
Came and it was time for it to mate we took it to a farm.
Every holiday without you will be terrible.
Every day it does not get better but worse.
Mother, poor thing, really cannot help herself at all.
She is exactly as she was: non-trusting, judgmental—everything I
    and she
Fought over—I am afraid that we will fight again . .
I don't want to, but she is asking for it. We love but—
You thought everything I did was perfect
She thinks I do nothing exactly as it should be
Difficult, difficult time.

I am not really trying to enjoy
Though I make all the right motions
Tonight in the car I explained to my daughter coming home from
Disneyland so late, I was really thinking about calling you, know-
ing you would
Be worried because we were so long . . and say we're home,
Daddy . . .
Knowing that I couldn't call you, I began to cry terribly
You see it is that thing
That special voice that I am used to
I remember when your father died and he was very old
We walked up the street and you, the huge man, were crying so
hard
You said to me, and I was about well maybe eighteen,
I am crying baby because a father is never old.
I never forgot that
For me you never were old, just with me longer.
It is all so unreal
Without any period to put to it
It isn't that I need to see you, though I do
It is that wonderful feeling you always gave me
Protected, secure, taken care of
That thing in you
Or is it with every daughter to every father? . . I bet it was so, in
their own
Way maybe they weren't lucky enough to have the kind of luxury
which we had

But there is something a father gives to a little girl whom he
    adores
And I guess I never grew up so I still need that . .
I can't describe it . . . it is just knowing that you were there
Always for me
And when the gods were not smiling
You would find a way to make them smile
You used to talk about pulling special strings and making things
    happen
And they did
Anyway, I thought, Daddy, . . . I thought it would be forever
And now as the days go by and the pieces of life rush to be put
    together
I ask myself over and over
Who will ever look at me the way you did.

When people talk to me it is so strange
They tell me I ought to be grateful that we had such a wonder-
    fulness for
Such a time
How lucky to have been loved like that
It only makes it worse
It only cuts deeper
It was not enough to have known it
I need to find a way not to need it
There will be no one to throw that vitamin into my soul
People love themselves too much for that
If I had known your time was up I would have told you the
    special
New things I kept putting off till later
Postponing telling you.
We always had so much to say to one another but I was hiding
    some
Things for a more propitious time
And why, being so close to you, did I not feel any of it
I knew there was peril
I knew fear and anger
But I did not know or smell death
I just blocked it
Why did I not know I ask myself
Why did I save till later what I needed to tell you
But maybe you knew and maybe you know
Wouldn't that be wonderful to believe death gives you
A special knowledge to know what I need you to know.

You see you really led me to believe in nothing
Led me and I followed so now while others have those special
    beliefs
I have nothing
Bad of you, don't you think?

If I were casting you in a play, who could play your part?
And all of those other things over and over, how did you ever
    make a
Living? I told my husband today that I hardly remember grade
    school
I was always going to somewhere at night and I remember little
    about
Being a girl in school.
I think I wasn't there too much because you thought I would get
    a better
Education at La Bohème
Maybe you were right
Were you Daddy?
Were you all I think you were?
No matter . . . you were right about La Bohème
I have needed it more than the square root of
Or what-pi-is or was
But with people Daddy I can talk about opera
It was a good choice.
I remember once going to an important Freudian analyst who
    said
I would have terrible trouble with men my own age if I didn't lose
My father feelings.

He was right
But the trouble wasn't terrible
Just often
But I think twenty years with one husband might prove the
  doctor
Wrong.
I remember going back and asking him what I ought to sub-
  stitute for you
And he sat puzzled saying. . .
Other things
I remember telling him if he found any answers to that
I would surely come back.
He never did
I never came back
Maybe he was right
Maybe they all were.
I doubt it though

Dear Daddy,

THE DAYS WILL FOLLOW INTO YEARS
AND I WILL LIVE A LONG TIME WITHOUT YOU
IF THE FATES ARE AS THEY SEEM
THAT WIVES LIVE LONGER THAN HUSBANDS
AND YOUNGEST CHILDREN LIVE LONGEST OF ALL
I WILL LIVE
I WILL HAVE YOU WITH ME EVERY MOMENT
FOR AS LONG AS I SEE A BLUEBIRD,
OR WASH A STRAWBERRY
OR SEE AN OLD MAN READING A JEWISH NEWSPAPER
OR SCREAM ABOUT SOME NATION'S FOREIGN POLICY
OR HEAR "HATIKVAH"
OR SEE A JEWISH FLAG
OR WATCH A SNOW
OR LOOK AT THE WALK OF MY SON . . .
OR SMILE AT THE CLEFT IN MY DAUGHTER'S CHIN
WHEN I GO TO THE THEATRE LOOKING ESPECIALLY
    SMASHING,
OR LOOK AT A MEMORIAL LIGHT IN A SYNAGOGUE
OR SEE A BOX OF CHOCOLATE-COVERED CHERRIES
OR HOLD A BLACK VELVET COAT NEXT TO ME
OR GET OFF A PLANE IN NEW YORK
OR LISTEN TO THE OPERA
OR TALK TO PEOPLE WHO HAVE COME FROM MIDDLE
    EUROPE
OR AVOID MY MOTHER'S DARKENED EYES . . .
AS LONG AS THERE IS LIFE INSIDE MY SOUL

I WILL REMEMBER
YOU GAVE ME THE JOY OF KNOWING I WAS SPECIAL
AND IN THAT KNOWLEDGE I WILL NEVER BE EMPTY
FOR I HAVE WALKED WITH A GIANT
AND SEEN THE GREAT MONUMENTS OF EUROPE WITH THAT
    LITTLE REFUGEE BOY
WHO CAME TO AMERICA SO THAT HIS FAMILY COULD HAVE
    A BETTER PART OF LIFE.
I WAS LUCKY THEN
I AM BLESSED NOW
I WILL NEVER BE ALONE

YOU WOULD NOT LEAVE ME UNPROTECTED
I WILL NEVER NEED TO FEAR
YOU ARE WATCHING OVER ME . . . . .

I KNOW IT